find it,
make it

find it, make it

35 step-by-step projects using found and natural materials

Clare Youngs

CICO BOOKS

LONDON NEW YORK

Published in 2011 by CICO Books
An imprint of
Ryland Peters & Small Ltd
20–21 Jockey's Fields   519 Broadway, 5th Floor
London WC1R 4BW   New York, NY 10012

www.cicobooks.com

10 9 8 7 6 5 4 3 2 1

A CIP catalog record for this book is available from the Library of Congress
and the British Library.

ISBN: 978 1 907563 05 8

Printed in China

Editor: Katie Hardwicke
Design: Jacqui Caulton
Photography: Claire Richardson
Styling: Clare Youngs

Contents

Introduction

Children always love collecting and gathering, but how often are there sandy buckets of shells and seaweed left outside from a seaside vacation, or how many times at the end of winter do you find bags full of withered conkers that are only fit for the trash? Well, no more! The abundance of found treasures collected on a woodland walk or a day spent on the beach can be transformed into the fun and imaginative projects in this book. Provide the space, some paint, and glue and the children will be occupied for hours. There is something for everyone—boys, girls, the very young, and the more experienced.

You won't have to go far to find materials that can be useful. Simply step outside your back door and you will be amazed at the amount of different materials you can gather to get crafting—from leaves and flowers, to pebbles and driftwood. Many of the projects will introduce your children to the traditional crafts of flower pressing, bark rubbing, and shell art, but although the crafts may be age old, the ideas are fresh, contemporary, and, most importantly, kids will have a great time making them.

All the projects are achievable with clear step instructions, but this book is not about making exact copies—it encourages imagination and experimentation. With a little guidance your children will be able to explore their own creative possibilities—their shells may not look like mice, they may look like dinosaurs! They may not be able to find a conker, so why not use a walnut shell instead? But whatever your children create, it will be unique and they will have had great fun planning and putting it together. A collecting expedition also makes for a great party activity. Give the children a check list and a bucket, and once they have found the necessary items show them how to make something that they can take home with them at the end of the day.

With so much talk about the environment these days, *Find It, Make It* also aims to encourage children to think more about the world they live in and recycling. Hopefully, by making the projects in this book, they will start thinking about the things around them and how they can be used in fresh, imaginative ways rather than always relying on store-bought materials. It's good to learn that shiny and new doesn't always mean it's the best. With a little creativity and care, even the everyday objects like twigs and stones can be turned into something exciting or attractive. Another great aspect of finding your own materials is that it's completely free, so what's not to love about it!

Many of the projects in this book give a child the opportunity to create a lasting memento of happy days on vacation or fun walks in the park. Encourage your children to keep a good lookout for oddly shaped sticks, pieces of fallen bark, pine cones, interesting pebbles and shells, and they will soon be making strange and wonderful animals and aliens, charming pieces of jewelry, beautiful artworks, and enchanting gifts. Getting your children to switch off the TV or computer and spend time outside connecting with nature has never been more fun!

Getting Ready

Basic crafting kit

Collecting materials

Basic crafting kit

Although the projects all contain materials that you find, there are a few key things that you will need before you start crafting at home.

Glue

There are lots of different types of glue. For many of the projects in this book you can use PVA (white craft glue). This is a very useful glue, that will stick most things. If you are sticking quite heavy items together you will need to leave them in position to dry before moving on to the next step. For some projects you will need to use stronger glue. Quick-drying all-purpose glue is ideal. It is a strong glue and young children should be supervised while using it. A glue stick is useful for sticking small flat items like leaves and flowers to paper.

Scissors

Always use safety scissors when cutting things for your projects. If you have to cut thick twigs or bark, ask an adult to help you.

Paints

I use acrylic paints for many of the projects in this book, but poster paints would work as well. Fabric inks are useful—just follow the manufacturer's instructions for setting the ink once you've applied your design. Have a selection of different colors of paint and then use an old plate as a mixing palette to create new ones. Keep a few used clean jars and yogurt pots: they make ideal water pots for when you need to clean your brush. A selection of brushes is useful, especially some thin brushes for painting details.

Pens and crayons

I like to use brush felt-tip pens for some projects. Sometimes these can be better than paints, especially on small items when it may be difficult to get a fine detail with a paintbrush. Wax crayons and pastels are great for bark and leaf rubbings.

String

A ball of string is very useful to have around as it can be used for all sorts of jobs—from tying sticks together to making legs for pinecone bugs. It comes in all sorts of colors, so pick a ball to match your favorite color scheme. Waxed beading thread is also available in a range of colors and the smooth, waxed coating makes it ideal for using with pendants or other jewelry.

Things to collect at home

It's a good idea to collect together a few household items that are useful to have on crafting days. As well as glue, scissors, paints, and paintbrushes, here are a few things that will always come in handy.

Newspaper and scrap paper

Some of the projects are going to get a little messy, particularly ones that involve paint. Mess is often part of the fun, but make sure you have a good supply of old newspaper to cover your work surface before you start. Alternatively, a wipeable plastic cloth is great for covering the table and can be used again and again. Also, keep a good supply of scrap paper to hand. Pick anything with an interesting pattern, such as pages in old magazines or gift wrap, as well as plain paper that can be turned into the flower paper on page 60.

Fabric and ribbons

Before getting rid of old clothes such as sweaters, t-shirts, and dresses, have a think about whether they could be cut up and used for something else. Start a sewing box where you can store all the pieces of fabric and ribbon you would like to re-use, then you can refer to it time and again to find the perfect scrap needed to make a project. Ribbons are particularly good to hold on to as they can be used for a number of things, whether it's hanging up a picture or decorating a gift.

Food

You'll be surprised by how many crafting materials you can find around the kitchen. Nut shells can be turned into all sorts of animals and people, so keep hold of a selection. Walnut shells are ideal for the baby bird nests on page 100, while the woodland folk on page 97 use peppercorns and dried pumpkins. Dried peas and lentils make handy eyes and noses, too. Small fruits can often be good for printing, and don't forget to save the whole peel from larger fruits to use as the base for a sailing boat, like the one on page 54.

Collecting materials

What to collect and when

Whenever you are out and about, keep your eyes peeled for suitable crafting materials. You will be amazed at the variety of natural treasures you can collect right outside your back door throughout the year.

Winter is usually a time when plants lay dormant, but there's still a lot out there to be found. One of the best things to look out for is fallen pieces of bark, as lots of trees develop white barks in interesting shapes that are great for bark rubbings (see page 34) or to make the bark bowl on page 42. Holly leaves are a great shape, so try a leaf print on some gift wrap (see page 76).

During the spring and summer months you will start to see a lot more flowers in the garden and out on walks in the woods. Leaves return to the trees and daisies and buttercups begin to appear. It's during this time that it's fun to get outside as the weather is perfect for collecting, whether you are planning a trip to the beach or just want to spend an hour having a hunt around the back yard. It's a good idea to collect some grasses and flowers at this time of year, then take them inside to let dry, so you can use them in future projects.

Autumn is a wonderful season to go foraging, as it is a real time for change in nature. The most noticeable thing is the change in color of the leaves, so collect as many as you can while you get the opportunity—you'll see some beautiful examples out there. This is a great time to make the woodland folk on page 97 as there are plenty of conkers, acorns, and seedpods to collect. Dandelions will also start to appear and will carry on growing right through winter.

There are many items you can collect all year round. You'll never be far from a good supply of twigs, and pebbles and stones are always available. Evergreen trees can provide you with pine cones and interesting leaves to use on printing projects and for your homemade paper (see page 60), while shells and sand can be gathered year-round at the beach.

Foraging essentials

On any foraging trip there are a few key items that you need to take with you. Firstly, make sure you dress correctly for the conditions outside. If it's been raining a lot, make sure you take a waterproof jacket and some wellies or boots so you don't slip over or get wet feet. Besides, it's always fun to jump in a few puddles when you're wrapped up in your waterproofs! If it's a hot day, put on a hat to keep the sun out of your face and make sure you put on some sun block.

You will also need something to carry your findings in. A bucket or a basket used for gardening are perfect for collecting things, but a bag will work equally well. Just make sure it's not brand new as it may get a little dirty!

Where to look

In the woods and the forest

An hour or two spent exploring the forest, or your local park, will guarantee a great haul of objects that can be made into animals, decorations, gifts, and more. One of the best items to collect are leaves, as they are very versatile and can be turned into any number of fun things to play with. Look out for colorful leaves that appear during the fall months, when the leaves turn beautiful shades of yellow and red. Smaller leaves are great for adding decorative detail to a project, whether you use them as a template for the Easter eggs (see page 46) or for leaf rubbings.

Keep your eyes peeled for pine cones and seed heads. They are particularly good for making into animals or figures as different-sized cones can be used for different body parts (see pages 89 and 105).

The other material that woodland has in abundance is twigs, you'll find them all over the place! Collect a bundle in a variety of different shapes and sizes and use them to spell out your name for the twig letters on page 30, or for the base of your raft on page 57. Look out for different types of grass growing in fields or ears of corn to use for the sun plaque on page 49.

In the garden or yard

The best thing about using recycled material is that there's a whole host of things just waiting to be found outside your bedroom window. The back yard is a great place to start and you'll find all kinds of things to use on future projects. Have a look at the flowers in the garden and see if there's anything suitable for the pressed flower butterfly (see page 24) or the daisy print bag (see page 71), but don't pick anything without an adult's permission as they might be growing them for a special purpose. Don't forget the weeds and grasses. Buttercups and daisies are ideal for pressing and are found in many gardens during the warmer months.

Keep an eye out for old flowerpots that can be brought to life with a little paint in the caterpillar flowerpots project on page 64 or the herb head flowerpots on page 86.

At home

Before you, or anybody else, throw things out at home, think about whether they could be of use for some of your future projects. Remember that orange you had at lunch? Well, keep the peel and give it a rinse, then use it for the fruity boats on page 54. And if you're looking for a sail for your boat, cut one from a plastic bag or an old sack. Empty jars are always good to keep hold of as well—not only are they ideal for storing seedpods, pretty shells, and more, but they make perfect containers for the lavender sugar on page 68.

Leaves from large house plants are also good and can be used to weave the palm leaf bowl on page 82, but check with an adult before you start pulling apart their prized pot plants! If you or your parents have been given a bunch of flowers, don't throw them away once they start to wilt: cut off the heads and leave them in a safe place to dry out, they can then be used for the flower family on page 89.

At the beach

A leisurely stroll along the seashore will reveal all sorts of useful bits and pieces to pick up. Shells are the key item to collect as they are an important material for a whole number of projects in the book, like the butterfly shell fridge magnets on page 50, the felt and shell bracelets on page 79, or the seashell mermaid on page 92. The beach is also a good place to find interesting pieces of driftwood. The sea often wears wood down to give it an attractive appearance that's ideal for the driftwood odd bunch (see page 94) or the box frame seaside scene (see page 33).

Think green

It's brilliant fun to go out collecting materials but remember to always respect nature and don't disrupt anything that shouldn't be tampered with. The environment is a fragile thing and taking something that's not supposed to be moved from its natural position can have a knock-on effect on the things around it. As a general rule, only take things from the ground, not from the trees. Flowers should not be picked from the wild, unless you happen across a field where they grow in abundance when it's OK to pick one or two. Be careful when picking up berries, nuts, or fruit as these may hide bugs and can sometimes be poisonous—always check with an adult before you collect them to avoid any potential problems. Stay away from mushrooms, as these can often be dangerous. When you are on the beach, don't take anything from rock pools—it's great fun to have a look and watch the plants and creatures that live there, but their home shouldn't be disturbed. Stick to the beach for collecting, there will be plenty of interesting things there.

Storing your finds

When you get home with your collection, it is a good idea to sort it out for storing. Wash and dry any pebbles or shells before you put them away. Old shoeboxes are ideal for storing larger items like twigs and leaves. Egg cartons are useful for collections of small shells and seedpods. Turn empty jars into great storage containers. Filled with pine cones, shells, or acorns, they can look very attractive displayed on a shelf.

Chapter One
Play and Display

Pressed flower butterfly

Pressing flowers is a lovely summertime activity. You could stick them into a scrapbook but I like to make something really special from them. This butterfly picture would make a wonderful present and you could make gift tags and cards to go with it from any leftover flowers. If you can't find any flowers to press, copy the templates on pages 115–116 and use those instead.

Materials

White or plain wooden picture frame
White acrylic paint (optional)
Paintbrush
Pressed flowers, petals, and leaves
Glue
Plain white paper
Scissors

1 If you have a plain wooden frame, paint the outer frame white. Make sure that your brushstrokes follow the direction of the grain of wood. Let dry.

2 When the paint is dry, lay some flowers or petals and leaves on the frame. Play around with the design and when you are happy with it, glue everything in place.

3 Trim a piece of white paper to fit the frame and arrange the remaining flowers and leaves on it in the shape of a butterfly.

4 When you are happy with the design, glue the pressed flowers in place. Carefully place the picture in the frame.

Words of wisdom

Pressing flowers is easy. Pick some flowers and leaves—don't pick wild flowers, only pick from your own garden and always ask permission first. Small, delicate flowers, such as pansies and daisies, work better than bulky big ones. You can also separate petals, such as rose petals. Make sure the flowers and leaves are dry and free from any crawling beasties! Flatten the flowers and lay them out on a piece of sugar paper. Cover with some more paper and place under a pile of books. It will take about two weeks before the flowers and leaves are dried and ready to use.

Printed fox wall hanging

Use leaves and twigs to create this unusual and stunning wall hanging. You can experiment with your collection of pine cones, seedpods, grasses, and leaves to make different marks. Try making other animal pictures, like a squirrel, or make a lovely hedgehog using a large leaf for the body and twigs for the prickles.

Materials

Template on page 117
Tracing paper and pencil
Scissors
Canvas
Fabric ink or paint in two
    toning colors
Paintbrush
Selection of leaves and twigs,
    pine cones, pebbles
Long stick for hanging
Double-sided tape
String

1 Using the template on page 117, draw out the three head sections onto some tracing paper. Cut out the sections and lay them down on a piece of canvas. Draw around each shape with a pencil.

2 Paint a small twig with fabric ink and carefully press it down on the paper to mark the outline of the head and nose, following the pencil guideline. Keep re-inking the twig as necessary. Take care not to smudge the wet paint.

3 Cut off the bottom quarter of a leaf and use the remainder as a print for the ear. Paint one side of the leaf with ink and press it onto the canvas, close to the edge of the fox's face. Repeat on the other side.

4 Take a smaller leaf and gently fold it in half. Cut a semicircle in the center of the leaf and unfold it to use as a template for the eye.

5 Paint one side of the leaf with ink and press it onto the paper to make two eye shapes.

6 Dip the end of a stick into some ink on a plate. Use the stick to fill the middle section of the fox's face by printing dots. Use two colors to create a pattern. Dip a pine cone in the ink and print a series of dots to fill in the inner area of the eye sections.

7 For the outer area of the eye, dip a thin twig in the ink and print a series of lines. Use the same twig to print some whiskers. To finish, use a pebble dipped in the ink to print a nose at the bottom of the face.

8 When the ink is dry, wrap the top edge of the canvas around a stick and secure with some double-sided tape. Tie a length of string to each end of the stick to make a hanging loop.

Twig letters

These brightly colored letters are a great way to personalize your own space. They would look brilliant on your bedroom door or above the bed, or make one for your best friend. They are also a fun way to decorate a present—wrap it in bright tissue paper and tie the recipient's initial to the parcel with a pretty ribbon.

Materials

Sticks
White paint
Paintbrushes
Paint in assorted bright colors
Glue

2 When the sticks are dry, paint a series of stripes down some sticks in a different color. Let dry.

3 Decorate the sticks further with alternate stripes in a different color or experiment with another pattern—stars, dots, flowers—the brighter the better!

4 Glue the sticks together to form the letters. Wait until the glue has completely dried before you display them on the wall.

1 Gather together some sticks of similar thicknesses. Break up the sticks to make different lengths and play around with them until you have arranged them in letter shapes. Paint the sticks white. You may need a couple of coats to get a good coverage. Try to keep the different sticks that belong to one letter together, or you may lose track of which stick belongs to which letter!

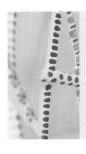

Words of wisdom

To make letters that are curved, like a C or a P, form the twigs into squares and triangles. For example, a "C" would be formed from three twigs, equal in length, stuck together to form three sides of a square. A "P" would be made with one twig for the upright section and two small twigs made into a triangle and placed toward the top of the upright twig.

Box frame seaside scene

A walk along the beach can turn up a host of interesting treasures. Besides the pebbles, shells, and seaweed, you can find smooth fragments of brightly colored glass, interesting pieces of string and rope, driftwood in all shapes and sizes, and, if you are very lucky, you may even find a fossil. A box frame is a lovely way to display your beachcombing finds. Painting little pictures onto the driftwood transforms a collection into a mini seaside scene.

Materials

Box frame
Paint: blue and white, plus assorted colors
Paintbrush
Beach finds: shells, seaweed, pebbles, sand, driftwood
Template on page 117, tracing paper, and pencil (optional)

1 Paint the outer frame in a pale blue. Remove the back of the frame and paint one side blue and white to represent the sky. Use blue as the base color and then apply streaks of white when it is dry.

2 Place the glass and border that come with the frame back into the outer frame. Start placing pebbles and shells along the bottom inside the frame. Remember that the ones at the bottom will be hidden by the frame and are just fillers. Place your favorite ones next to the glass, as these are the ones that will show. Fill up with little stones and sand to about halfway up the frame.

3 Paint some seaside scenes onto small pieces of driftwood. You could paint beach huts, seagulls, deckchairs, beach umbrellas, or little sailing boats. If you wish, use the template on page 117. Let dry.

4 Position the driftwood pieces by pushing them down into the layer of pebbles. Replace the back of the frame and secure it in place. Be careful as you stand it upright, as the pebbles and sand will shift slightly as it settles.

Bark rubbing picture and twig frame

You can get wonderful effects and textures by using oil pastels or wax crayons to make bark and leaf rubbings. Use lots of bright colors and then cut them up into different shapes to make vibrant works of art. Your picture will look stunning surrounded by a stylish white twig frame.

Materials

White or plain wooden frame
Selection of small twigs
White acrylic paint
Paintbrush
Glue
Colored paper for background
Thin white paper
Scissors
Piece of bark and small leaves
Oil pastels or wax crayons in assorted colors
Template on page 118, tracing paper, and pencil (optional)
Glue stick

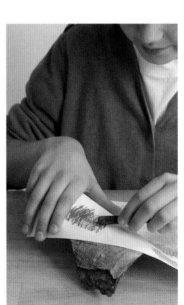

1 Prepare the frame. Coat your twigs with white acrylic paint and let dry. If you have a wooden frame, give your frame a couple of coats of white paint, too. Arrange the twigs all around the frame and glue in place. Put aside to dry.

2 Prepare your background paper. Trace around the backing piece for the frame onto your colored paper and cut it out.

3 Put a sheet of thin white paper over the piece of bark and make bark rubbings using different colored crayons. You can either do this at a table with a piece of bark that you have found, or go outside and take the rubbings straight from the trees.

4 Using a clean piece of white paper, rub over the small leaves with a green crayon and then cut out the leaf shapes.

5 Trace the template on page 118 and cut different-colored shapes from the bark rubbings to make up the bird—cut out a body, wings, legs, beak, and eyes.

6 Arrange the bird pieces on the colored background paper and glue in place. Draw in an eye with a matching crayon.

7 To finish, glue a small twig beneath the bird's feet and add the paper leaves to the end. Place the finished picture in the frame.

Hanging bird decoration

Flat shells work best for this project, but experiment with different-shaped shells that you have collected. I have hung them from a ribbon to make a garland but they can also hang individually. Try painting some twigs white and suspend the birds from the branches for a charming table decoration.

Materials

Colored paper, such as recycled
  gift wrap
Template on page 117, tracing
  paper, and pencil (optional)
Scissors
Flat shells
Small leaves and twigs
Thick paper or card
Glue
String or thin ribbon

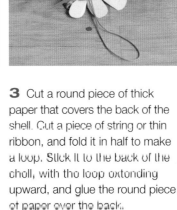

1 Cut out three thin oval shapes from scraps of colored paper for the wings. Cut out a beak shape, an eye, and trim two twigs to the same length for the legs. You may wish to use the templates on page 117.

2 Glue the wings, legs, and beak onto the back of the shell, fan out the wings across the top of the bird's "body." Let dry.

3 Cut a round piece of thick paper that covers the back of the shell. Cut a piece of string or thin ribbon, and fold it in half to make a loop. Stick it to the back of the shell, with the loop extending upward, and glue the round piece of paper over the back.

4 Finally, glue a leaf onto the front as a wing and stick the eye in position. When everything is dry, you can hang your bird from the nearest branch.

Froggy bookends

Transform a few pebbles into this happy smiley frog with a little paint and glue. Make two and you have a pair of bookends! The pebbles will be quite heavy, so once they have been glued together, make sure you leave them to dry completely.

Materials

One large flat pebble
One thin, wide pebble
Two small wide pebbles
Paint in assorted colors
Small paintbrush
Glue
Varnish (optional)

1 Check that your pebbles are clean and dry. Paint some flowers or dots around the larger pebble for the frog's body.

2 Paint the thin, wide pebble with a base coat of green. Let dry and then paint on a wide smiley mouth in a darker color.

3 To make the eyes, paint a white circle onto the small pebbles and, when dry, add a black dot in the center of each circle.

4 Glue the mouth section to the body and then glue the two eyes in position. You may have to hold the pebbles in place while the glue starts to set. If you like, you can give your frog a coat of varnish to give him a nice shine.

Words of wisdom

You could use the same combination of pebbles as for the frog to make a monkey by painting it in a different way. Start by painting the stones brown, then draw a line for the mouth along the bottom pebble and two eyes on the middle pebble. To finish, draw two semicircles at the base of the two small pebbles at the top to make the ears.

Aboriginal bark bowl

This little lizard is painted in the style of Aboriginal dot paintings. In Australia, they paint on the bark from a stringybark tree. Some of the colors traditionally used were made from colored rocks ground to a powder with liquid added. The design is marked out with the end of a stick. While on walks in the park or woods, look out for any suitable pieces of bark on the ground. Even tiny pieces can be made into something decorative and useful. Try designing your own patterns—a fish or a snake shape would work very well—and mark them out on the wood with the end of a stick or pencil.

Materials

Template on page 120
Tracing paper and pencil
Scissors
Piece of bark
At least 3 small sticks with
    different-shaped ends (such
    as a pencil, paintbrush,
    wooden clothes pin,
    wooden spoon)
White paint
Paint in contrast colors

1 Using the lizard template on page 120, copy the design onto tracing paper with a pencil and cut it out.

2 Place the template on the smooth side of your bark piece. Draw around the template in pencil and then transfer the markings onto the piece of wood.

3 Take a small stick and dip it in the white paint. Apply dots to the pencil lines on the bark to create a pattern for the body.

4 Dip a thin stick into the paint and mark out the legs, feet, and tongue. Finish by decorating the body with paint in a different, contrast color. Use different shaped sticks to vary the pattern.

Words of wisdom

Try using sticks with different-shaped ends to give different effects. For example, a wooden clothes pin removed from the wire makes a nice oblong shape.

Wind chime

Hang this pretty wind chime in the garden, in a window, or even as an indoor mobile, and listen to the gentle clink of shells in the breeze. If you can't get hold of colored raffia, you can color in plain raffia with felt-tip pens, or tie the shells together with brightly colored ribbon.

Materials

Raffia
Scissors
Shells
Long stick for hanging

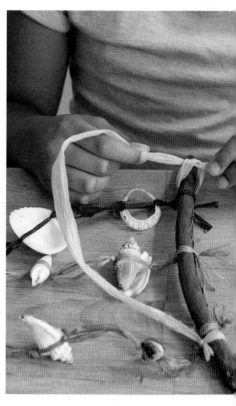

1 To make one strand, cut two lengths of raffia about 18in (45cm) long. Tie them together with a knot about 2¼in (6cm) from one end.

2 Tie on some shells, spacing them evenly along the strand. Make sure that the shell is tied on tightly, with knots holding it in place on either side.

3 Tie a knot about 2in (5cm) above the last shell. Tie the strand onto the stick.

4 Make up two more strands in the same way, using different colored raffia. Tie the separate strands onto the stick, spacing them evenly. Trim the ends. Tie a piece of raffia to each end of the stick to make a loop for hanging.

Words of wisdom

Other beachcombing finds, such as small pebbles or pieces of worn, smooth glass in jewel colors, would also make a pretty wind chime full of seaside memories.

Leaf print Easter eggs

This project is a lovely way to capture the amazing varieties of leaf shapes. Ferns and groups of small, delicate leaves work well, and the feathery sprigs of dill and fennel are particularly pretty. The eggs are colored with a little food coloring—try delicate pastel colors for a charming Easter display.

Materials

A few sprigs of small leaves, such as ferns, dill, fennel
White eggs (large eggs or duck eggs work well)
Old pair of pantyhose (tights)
Elastic bands
Food coloring
Cup and spoon

1 Choose a leaf and lay it on the egg in the position you would like. Cut a small section from an old pair of pantyhose. Position the fabric over the egg and leaf, and gather it together at the back. Make sure the leaf is flat and the fabric is smooth and covers the whole egg.

2 Secure the gathered piece of pantyhose with an elastic band wound around tightly to hold everything in place.

3 Fill a cup with water. Add a few drops of food coloring to the cup and stir to mix well.

4 Lower the egg into the cup. Leave for a few minutes for the dye to take. If you want a stronger color, use more coloring and leave the egg in the cup for longer.

5 When you have finished dyeing the egg, lift it out using the gathered knot. Remove the elastic band, fabric, and leaf to reveal your design. Let dry before displaying.

Words of wisdom

If you want to keep your eggs to display the following year, you will have to blow them. You may need to ask an adult to help. Using a needle, prick a small hole in one end of the egg and a slightly larger hole at the other end. Push the needle into the egg to break the yolk. Blow out the egg (the white and yolk) through the larger hole—don't suck! Place the empty eggshell under running water to gently clean the inside.

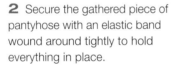

Sun plaque

You may think of grass as rather ordinary but really it is quite a special plant, with a huge variety of colors and shapes. When you are next on a country walk, see how many different types you can spot. Here, I've combined dried grass stalks with clay to make a glowing sun plaque to brighten any wall.

Materials

Clay
Rolling pin
Round cutter
Grasses, wheat, or ripened corn
   ears, seeds, acorns
Paintbrush or pencil
Ribbon

1 Roll out a piece of clay until it measures about ½in (10mm) thick. Use a pastry cutter or a glass to press out a circle.

2 Press seeds, the tops of acorns, or bits of grass into the circle to make the eyes, mouth, nose, and cheeks.

3 Trim the grass stalks to similar lengths then push the stalks in all around the outer edge of the circle to make the sun's rays. Use shorter stalks to fill the gaps.

4 Poke the end of a paintbrush or pencil through the top of the plaque to make a hanging hole, then leave the plaque to dry. When the clay is dry you can thread a ribbon through to hang your plaque.

Words of wisdom

The face is made from clay. In our garden, you can dig down and the earth becomes clay—not so good for gardening, but great for crafting! Don't worry if you don't have clay in your garden as you can buy it at an art or craft supply store.

Butterfly shell fridge magnets

Sometimes when scouring the beach for shells you may be lucky and find a complete two-sided shell. You can turn this into a pretty butterfly fridge magnet. Don't worry if you can't find one, as you can stick two similar shells next to each other but you may need a larger-sized magnet to attach them to.

Materials

Shells
Paint: white and assorted colors
Small paintbrush
Small magnet
Glue

2 Paint butterfly wings or a simple pattern on each side of the shells. Try to make the two sides symmetrical.

3 Once you are happy with the pattern, carefully paint the body of the butterfly between the shells and add the antennae.

4 When the paint is dry, stick the magnet to the back of the shells with a small dot of glue and let dry.

1 Wash the shells in hot, soapy water and dry them carefully. When completely dry, give the shells a base coat of white paint. Let dry.

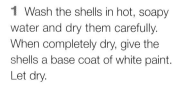

Chapter Two
Playtime!

Fruity boats

These little colorful fruit boats are so simple to make—and once you have scooped out the fruit you can make a refreshing fruit salad! I love to recycle and have used the pretty tissue paper that is sometimes wrapped around the fruit to make the sails, but you could use scraps of gift wrap, candy wrappers, or old postcards and envelopes.

Materials

Fruit, such as melon, avocado, pineapple, mango, orange
Spoon
Leafy stalks or twigs
Small piece of modeling clay
Scissors
Scraps of paper or tissue

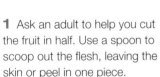

1 Ask an adult to help you cut the fruit in half. Use a spoon to scoop out the flesh, leaving the skin or peel in one piece.

2 Strip the lower leaves from your leaf stalk or twig, leaving some in place at the top to act as a flag.

3 Cut out a sail from your scraps of paper or tissue. You can make it an oblong or a triangle. Push the lower end of a twig through the paper sail near the top and then out again further down the sail.

4 Place a small ball of modeling clay in the bottom of the fruit half. Push the end of the sail into the clay—you're ready to launch.

Twig raft

From simple leaf and twig rafts to more elaborately constructed sailing boats, there is something very satisfying about launching and watching a homemade vessel float on the water. When you have finished sailing your raft, it would look lovely sitting on a shelf in the bathroom or your bedroom.

Materials

Straight, thin sticks or twigs,
  such as willow
String
Scissors
Small scrap of sacking
Leaf
Small ball of modeling clay

1 Break some thin sticks into equal lengths about 8in (20cm) long, or to the size you want. Lay some sticks alongside each other to your required width. Cut three lengths of string four times the width of the raft. Fold the first piece of string in half and loop it around the first stick about a third of the way along the raft.

2 Place the next stick alongside it. Twist the string, placing one piece over the other and then loop it around the next stick.

3 Continue to add the sticks as in Step 2. Finish with a double knot and trim off the ends.

4 Repeat Steps 2 and 3 with the remaining two pieces of string, keeping the distance between each section roughly the same.

Words of wisdom

You might have to experiment with the position of the modeling clay in order to get the raft to balance correctly. If one side of the boat always sinks into the water there is too much weight on that side. Add a bit more clay to the opposite side of the raft and test it in the water. If it's still unbalanced, add a little more clay until you get the perfect weight distribution.

5 Cut out an oblong of sacking material—I used an old coffee sack that had some great printed letters and numbers on it. Push a twig through the material to form a sail.

6 Cut a flag shape from a large leaf, or use a complete leaf. Push the top of the stick through the leaf to form the flag.

7 To attach the sail to the raft, put a small ball of modeling clay on the base of the raft in the center, and press the mast into it to secure. You're now ready to face the rapids!

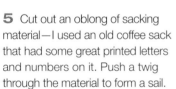

Leaf and flower paper

There is something very special about handmade paper and it is actually very easy to make. Once you've made one batch, you can build up a collection and make a huge variety of seasonal papers by adding flower petals, leaves, and seeds throughout the year.

Materials

Scrap paper
Blender
Water
Washing-up bowl
Embroidery frame
Piece of cheesecloth (muslin) or tulle fabric
Flat leaves, flowers, and seeds
Spoon
Towel
Hole punch (optional)
Ribbon (optional)

1 Start by making a paper pulp. Tear up some scraps of paper into small pieces and put them in a blender until half full. Pour in enough water so that the blender is three-quarters full. Ask an adult to help you to whizz the mixture until you have a pulp.

2 Pour the paper pulp into a large bowl, such as a washing-up bowl. Add 2 pitchers of water, approximately 3½ pints (2 litres), and mix it all around with your hands. It's very messy!

3 Separate the two sections of the embroidery frame. Lay a piece of fine fabric, such as cheesecloth (muslin) or tulle, over the smaller section and measure and cut a square approximately 1¼in (3cm) larger than the frame.

4 Place the larger section of the embroidery frame over the smaller and tighten. Try not to push the two sections together so that they are level with each other, but leave the outer frame slightly raised above the smaller one.

5 Now for the fun bit! Swish your hands around in the water so that the pulp is evenly distributed. Dip the frame down away from you and lower it into the water at an angle. Straighten it up under the water and then slowly bring it out. Let the water drip through.

6 Rest the frame on the side of the bowl and position your leaves, flowers, or seeds on top. Pour some of the pulp mixture over the flowers and leaves using a spoon.

7 Gently place the frame on a towel, remove the frame, and let dry for several hours or overnight. The next day it should be dry and you can carefully peel the paper away from the fabric.

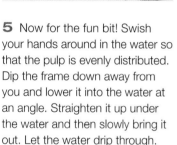

Words of wisdom

There are so many uses for handmade paper: cut out simple shapes like flowers, birds, or butterflies (see opposite), punch a hole in the paper and thread a piece of ribbon through to make pretty gift labels; cut out oblongs to use as special writing paper; or fold the oblong in half to make notelets, ideal for thank-you notes. You could also divide the oblongs into thin strips to make original bookmarks for your friends.

8 To make a notebook, cut out some oblongs from the paper circle to make a front and back cover. Cut some plain paper the same size for the inside of the book. Punch holes through all the layers, thread some ribbon through, and tie together. Use any trimmings to make gift tags.

Caterpillar flowerpots

This is a lovely way to use all the little pebbles you picked up at the beach and would be a great project for a craft-themed party. Use popsicle sticks to make name tags, so everyone knows which is their pot at going home time.

Materials

Small clay flowerpot
White paint
Paintbrush
Small round pebbles
Glue
3D puffa paint in assorted colors
Thin stick
Popsicle stick
Pens
Shell
Plant and potting compost

1 Paint the outside of the flowerpot white. You can leave the rim unpainted for contrast if you like. Let dry.

2 Glue some pebbles around the pot at different heights, with a small gap between each one, to make the caterpillar's body.

3 Use 3D puffa paints to draw a circle around each pebble to join them up and make the caterpillar.

4 Dip a thin stick into the paint and mark out some legs, feet, and tongue. Finish with some different-colored paint to decorate the body.

5 Draw a snail body onto a popsicle stick and glue on a small shell to complete the snail. When everything is dry, pot up your plant and add the popsicle stick label.

Chapter Three
Gift Ideas and Jewelry

Lavender sugar

Lavender has been used as a flavoring in cooking for hundreds of years. It has a strong taste but if you add just a little to some sugar it makes a wonderful, gently fragrant mix that you can use when making cakes or sprinkle over homemade cookies. Make sure the lavender you pick has not been sprayed with a pesticide.

Materials

(for one 12oz/340g jar)

A few sprigs of fresh lavender
½ cup (115g) superfine (caster) sugar
Mixing bowl and spoon
Glass jar with lid
Patterned paper
Scissors
Ribbon

1 Take a few sprigs of lavender and remove the little flower heads until you have gathered about 1 dessertspoon. Try to pick just the purple part and throw away any brown bits.

2 Put the sugar in a bowl and add the lavender flowers. Mix them together well with a spoon.

3 Scoop the sugar mixture into a clean, dry jar using a spoon. Screw on the lid.

4 To decorate your jar, place a saucer on some pretty paper, draw around it, and cut out the circle. Put the circle over the jar lid and tie it in place with a ribbon.

Daisy print bag

This project is a lovely activity to have at a party, and when it's time to go home you have a party bag and party favor all in one! Plain calico bags can be found at most craft stores or online, ready to be decorated with pretty patterns, or you could adapt the design to print onto a plain white t-shirt instead.

Materials

Selection of twigs, flowers, and leaves
Fabric ink in at least 3 colors
Paintbrush
Plain calico bag
Template on page 121, tracing paper, and pencil (optional)

1 Paint fabric ink onto a thin twig and place it vertically on the center of the bag, with the bottom of the twig aligned with the base of the bag. Press down evenly along the twig and then carefully lift it off. If you wish, use the template on page 121 to help make the flower shape. If you wish, use the template on page 121 to help make the flower shape.

2 Print two more stalks on either side of the first one. Try to keep the spaces in between the middle stalk and the edge of the bag even. Paint one side of a leaf with green fabric ink and press down twice on each side of each printed stalk.

3 Paint a flower with fabric ink and press it face down at the top of the stalk. Make sure that all the petals make contact with the fabric in order to give you a clear print. Repeat with a fresh flower and different color for the remaining stalks.

4 Use small leaves to print a pattern in contrasting colors along the top and bottom edges of the bag and along the straps. Follow the manufacturer's instructions for setting the fabric ink.

Words of wisdom

Bear in mind that your flower will need to be quite robust in order to keep its shape when printing. I have used a large daisy flower as this is a good shape to print and it doesn't fall apart easily once you've applied the paint.

Slate brooch

These charming brooches are made from little pieces of slate, which is often used as a decorative covering in gardens. Choose a rounded piece that is thin and light and has no sharp edges. You can paint anything you like on your brooch but I think wildlife, like hedgehogs or little birds, looks great with the natural color of the slate.

1 Paint a base coat of metallic paint in the shape of a hedgehog or your chosen design onto the slate piece.

2 When the metallic paint is dry, paint some white bristles or other decoration on top of the design. If you wish, use the template on page 120 as a guide to draw a bird.

3 With a black marker pen, build up your design by adding some more bristles and an eye and nose.

4 Glue an old button badge onto the back of the slate as a fastener. Let dry thoroughly before wearing.

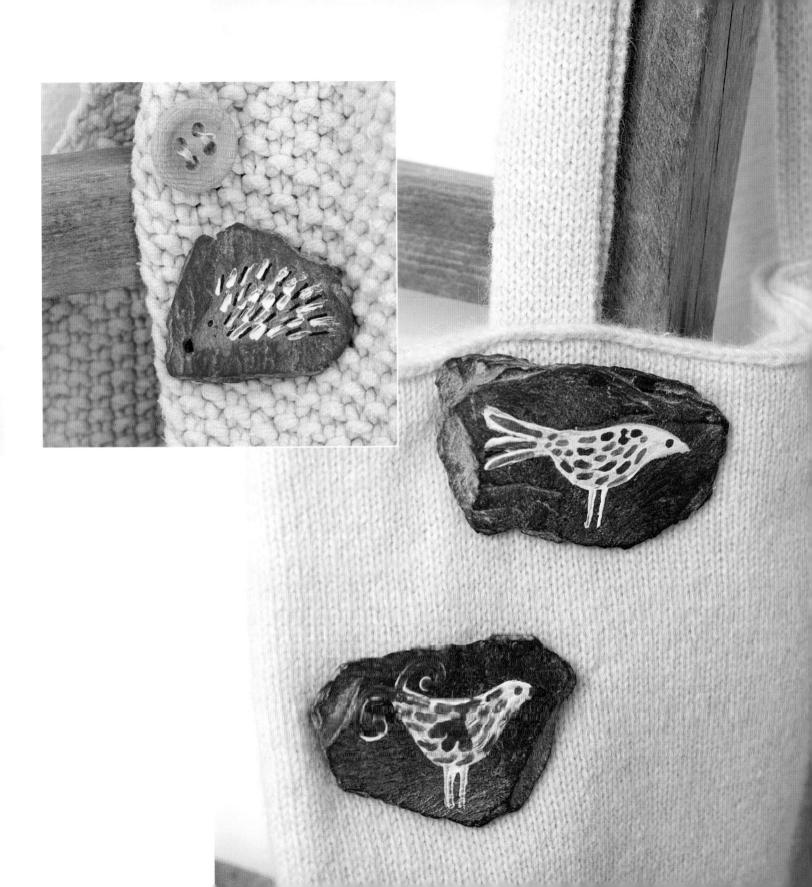

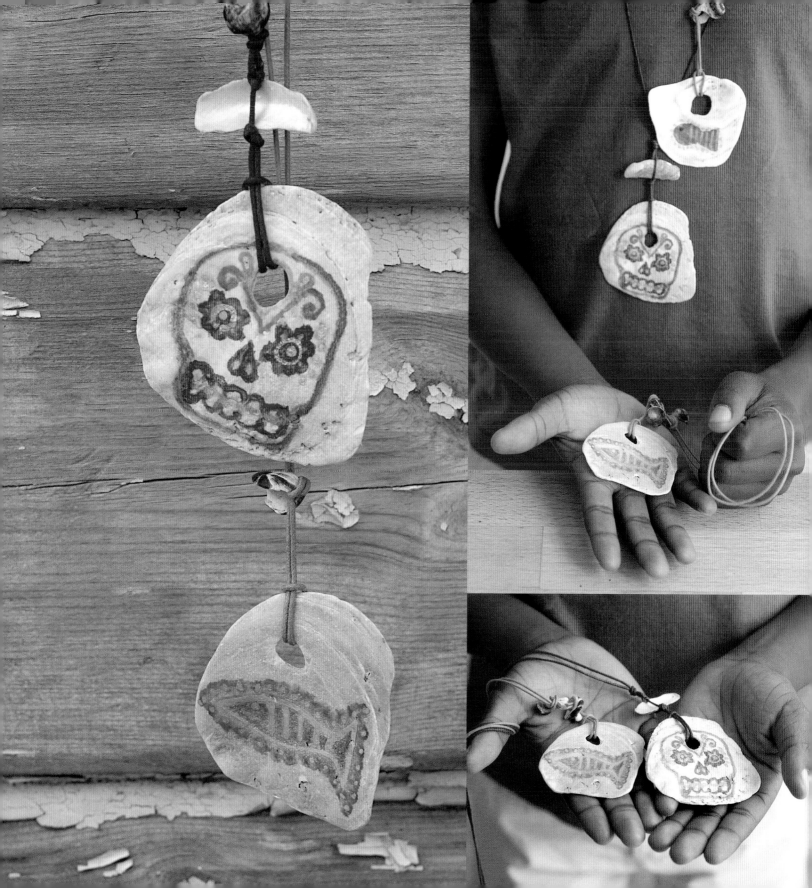

Shell pendant

When looking for shells and pebbles on the beach, see if you can find ones with holes in as they make wonderful necklaces or pendants. I found these large flat oyster shells that are perfect for painting. You may find a pebble that you could use, as long as it is not too heavy. Try out different designs: fish or little boats work well, and this brightly colored skull is based on Mexican folk art.

Materials

Flat shells or pebbles with holes
Felt-tip pens or paints in assorted colors
Metallic gold or silver pen
Waxed cotton beading thread

1 Make sure your shell is clean and dry. Paint or draw a design onto your shell – a bold shape will stand out clearly. (You may wish to use the templates on page 121.)

2 Embellish your design further if you wish. Some decoration using a metallic pen will add an extra bit of sparkle.

3 Cut a piece of waxed cotton thread long enough to go easily over your head and with about 1½in (4cm) extra for tying knots. Fold the thread in half and thread the two ends through the hole in the shell and back through the loop in the thread. Pull tightly to secure.

4 Thread on a couple of small shells with holes and tie in place along the pendant. Tie the two ends of the thread together to finish the pendant to the required length.

Fern print gift wrap and garland

The delicate and pretty fronds of a fern plant are perfect for printing with, transforming ordinary brown paper into gorgeous gift wrap. For the little bird tag, I used some bark that had been shed from a silver birch tree, but if you can't find any, you could use dried leaves or a section from your printed wrap.

Materials

Kitchen paper towel
Fern leaves
Paint in assorted colors
Paintbrush
Brown paper wrap
Little pine cones, acorns, or
    seedheads
Raffia
Thin bark
Thin card
Glue
Template on page 121
Tracing paper and pencil
Scissors
Hole punch

1 Place some fern leaves on top of a piece of kitchen paper towel. Cover one side of the fern leaves with paint.

2 Put the painted fern leaf in position, paint side down on the brown paper. Press down carefully, trying to make sure that all the bits of the fern make contact with the paper. Make a few more prints, overlaying colors for different effects, until you are happy with the design. Let dry.

3 To make the garland, simply tie some pine cones, acorns, or seedheads to some brightly colored raffia, spacing them evenly along the length.

4 To make the tag, stick a piece of bark to some thin card. Trace the bird shape from the template on page 121 and cut it out. Lay it on the bark and card and draw around it.

5 Cut out the bird and punch a hole for the eye. Thread the bird tag onto the raffia garland.

Felt and shell bracelets

It is always lovely to find complete shells along the beach, but I also love collecting tiny fragments of shells that have been worn smooth by the sea. There is a huge variety of colors—from pearly pinks and oranges to the rich hues of blues and purples. Placed together in a row, they make a pretty and very unusual bracelet. Make one for a special friend; it would be a charming gift—you could also make little brooches and rings and have a whole collection of jewelry.

Materials

Felt
Scissors
Fragments of shells
Small shell for fastening
Sewing needle and thread

1 Cut a strip of felt about ⅝in (1.5cm) wide. For the length, wrap the strip around your wrist and add about ¾in (2cm) overlap before trimming it to fit.

2 Sew on the shell fragments by crossing the thread over the shell from one side to the other, so it forms a starlike pattern over the shell. Start the first fragment ⅝in (1.5cm) from one end, space the shells evenly, and leave ¾in (2cm) spare at the other end.

3 Fold the ¾in (2cm) end over and snip a little slit in the center of the felt. Try not to get the slit too near the edge.

4 Finally, sew on a little shell on the opposite end to the slit, as the fastening button.

Flower ice bowl

Water and fresh flowers are all it takes to make this gorgeous bowl. Fill it with fruit or little homemade popsicles as the centerpiece on a summer party table. Your friends will be stunned and think you are amazingly clever when they realize it is made only from water.

Materials

2 round bowls, one approximately ¾in (2cm) smaller in diameter than the other
Pitcher of water
Selection of fresh flowers and leaves
Weight, such as a stone or can

1 Pour water into a bowl to a depth of 1in (2.5cm). Place it in the freezer until it has frozen solid—this usually takes one or two hours.

2 Once the first layer has frozen, place the smaller bowl inside the larger bowl. Take some clean flowers and leaves and position them in the gap between the two bowls.

3 Once the whole area between the two bowls has been filled with flowers, carefully pour water into the gap until it reaches the edge of the bowls, poking down any flowers that stick out of the top.

4 You may find the bowl will start to float, so weigh it down with a stone or can and then place it in the freezer for a few hours. Take it out about 15 minutes before you need it. This will cause it to melt slightly, making it easier to remove the inner and outer bowls.

Words of wisdom

Everyone loves a popsicle or ice lolly on a hot summer's day, so why not make a giant bowl-shaped one to share with friends? Try using some fruit juice and a selection of berries instead of water before putting it in the freezer to set.

Palm leaf bowl

Tropical-type plants are very popular as house plants and in gardens today. You may have one in your garden that has long, thin leaves which you can use to make this clever bowl. Serve some fruit piled on one of these bowls at a summer picnic for something really special.

Materials

Long, thin leaves, such as
    palm leaves
Scissors
Paperclips
Raffia

1 Decide how long you want your bowl to be and cut some leaves to this length. Cut down either side of the tough central stalk so that you have two equal pieces from one leaf. Discard the stalk.

2 Lay four leaf strips next to each other and start weaving some across. Remember, if you start the first one by going under the lengthwise strips, then the next one should start off by going over the top.

3 Continue until you have woven about five or six strips, depending on the length of your bowl. Place the strips about ¾in (2cm) apart.

4 Trim the horizontal (crosswise) strips so that they extend about 1½in (4cm) on either side. Bend these strips back into the bowl and tuck the ends in to secure. Ensure that the horizontal leaf bends right around the edge of the lengthwise strips.

5 Gather the long ends together using a paperclip to hold them in place while you tie the strips together with some brightly colored raffia. Remove the paperclip and trim the ends of the raffia to neaten them.

Chapter Four
Colorful Characters

Herb head flowerpots

Materials

Paint in assorted colors
Paintbrush
Flowerpot
Varnish
Pebbles
Potting compost
Seeds

It is great fun to help out in the kitchen and get involved with the cooking. There is no better way to eat healthily than to grow your own! Make a mini herb garden for the kitchen windowsill and all you budding chefs can experiment with different flavors in your recipes. Line up the flowerpots and paint a row of different faces, then grow some crazy, but tasty, hairstyles!

1 Paint a face shape onto the front of the flowerpot. Make sure the face goes all the way up to the top edge of the pot.

2 Decorate the face shape with some eyes, a nose, and a mouth, even a pair of glasses if you like. When the paint has dried, you can give the pot a coat of varnish to make the paint more hard-wearing, but it is not essential.

3 Place a couple of small pebbles at the bottom of the pot to help it to drain and then carefully fill it up with some potting compost until it is about three-quarters full.

1 Sprinkle some herb seeds on the surface. If you are using cress seeds you do not need any more potting compost on top. For other herbs, add a very thin covering of compost. Position in a sunny spot and remember to water your seedlings as the "hair" starts to sprout.

Words of wisdom

For instant hair, plant small herb plants bought from the garden center in the pots.

Herb Head Flowerpots **87**

Flower family

These delicate and enchanting little people are made from dried grasses and flowers, which you can dry yourself. Some flowers work better than others, so it is worth experimenting. With a little colored raffia and your imagination, you'll soon have your own flower folk to hide at the bottom of the garden!

Materials

Selection of dried flowers, grasses, pine needles, seedpods, bark
Scissors
Raffia in assorted colors
Template on page 122
Glue
Tracing paper and pencil
White pencil

1 To make the lady, use a dried flower that has petals for the skirt and a flower or seedpod that would make a suitable head. Leave approximately 1¼in (3cm) of the stem on the flower and head, and tie them together with a little raffia.

2 Wind the raffia around to form the body, leaving two lengths of raffia sticking out each side for the arms. Tie a knot at each end for the hands.

3 Push some small twigs into the flower skirt to make the legs. You may need some glue to secure them.

4 To make the man, I used some pine needles still attached to the twig. Separate the needles into two bunches to make the legs. Tie off the bottom bits and trim to make the feet.

Words of wisdom

Drying flowers is really easy. Tie a few flowers together at the bottom of the stems, in small bunches. Hang them upside down somewhere dark and warm—the back of a closet would work well. Leave them for 3 or 4 weeks until the flowers have completely dried out.

5 Tie some raffia around the top of the pine needle bunch to make some arms, knotting the ends as you did for tho lady in Stop 2.

6 Wrap the bundle with different colored raffia to make the body and stick a flower or seedpod onto the body to make the head.

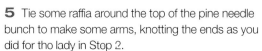

7 Io make the dog, copy the template on page 122 and draw onto a thin piece of bark using a white pencil.

8 Carefully cut the dog out of the bark and tle a piece of raffia around it for the leash.

Seashell mermaid

I always come back from a beach walk with a pocket full of shells. Sometimes, a while later, I dip my hand in a jacket pocket and discover them still there—holding them brings back lovely memories of shoreline walks. Here is a way of using your shells to make a unique work of art that would look lovely on a bathroom shelf or placed among pots and plants as an unusual garden ornament.

Materials

Piece of wood or driftwood to fit the mermaid template, with some space to spare
White acrylic paint
Paintbrush
Cloth
Template on page 123
Tracing paper and pencil
Scissors
Shells
Paints or felt-tip pens in assorted colors
Glue

1 Paint a piece of wood with thin white acrylic paint. Use a damp cloth to rub some of the paint off while it is still wet to give the background a faded, seaside look. Trace the mermaid template on page 123 onto tracing paper. Cut out and position it on the wood. Draw around the outline with a pencil.

2 Choose a shell that would make a suitable face. Paint or draw on eyes, nose, mouth, and rosy cheeks. Glue in position.

3 Arrange your shells to fill in the areas for the hair, body, and tail. When you are happy with your arrangement, paint glue onto the wood and stick the shells in place.

4 Add some small shells for the arms and finally stick some shells around the edge to make a border.

Words of wisdom

While on your beach walk, look out for suitable pieces of driftwood to make the base for your mermaid picture.

Driftwood odd bunch

Materials

Pieces of driftwood
Glue
Acrylic paint in assorted
  colors
Paintbrush
String or rope

On walks along the beach keep a look out for bits of driftwood. An interesting shape, smoothed and weathered by the sea, can be a thing of beauty in itself. Smaller pieces can be put together to make sculptures. Gather some pieces and when you get them home, look at each piece of wood, turning it this way and that—you may see the head of an alien in one piece, a pair of legs in another. Start placing bits together to make a figure or animal. Each one will have a character of its own and be totally unique.

1 Play around with different bits of wood until you are happy with your arrangement. Glue the pieces of wood together. You may have to hold them in position for a few moments as the glue dries.

2 Apply a base coat of white acrylic paint, or another color, to your design and let dry before adding further colors on top.

3 Use acrylic paints to paint on the eyes and mouth. Use bright colors to paint the body. I think it looks good to leave some of the wood showing.

4 You can use any string or rope that you may have found for arms or legs. Glue in position and let dry before you play with your odd bunch creature.

Woodland folk

The fall is the best season for foraging—the ground is covered with fallen leaves in rich reds and oranges, the gardens and hedgerows are full of berries and seedpods, and there are acorns, pine cones, and grasses to collect. Who can resist picking up beautiful shiny new conkers? Capture the fall bounty in these cute little folk. I have used a mini dried pumpkin for the head but a conker would work very well or an acorn with a ready-made hat!

Materials

Paint in assorted colors
Small paintbrush
Mini dried pumpkin, conker,
    or acorn
Red peppercorns or beads
Pine cone
Glue
Waxed beading thread or string
Scissors
Wooden basket, moss,
    ribbon (optional)

1 Using a small paintbrush, paint a face onto the head. Glue on a red peppercorn or bead for a nose.

2 Stick on the body—I have used a little pine cone. Let the glue dry. Cut two lengths of waxed beading thread or string, one piece to make the arms and one piece to make the legs.

3 Stick a red peppercorn or a bead at each end of the string to make the hands and feet and then glue the arms and legs to the body. Let dry.

4 To keep your woodland folk safe, you could provide them with a little basket. Fill with dried moss and decorate with ribbon or dried leaves, then place your little folk inside for all to see.

Chapter Five
Amazing Animals

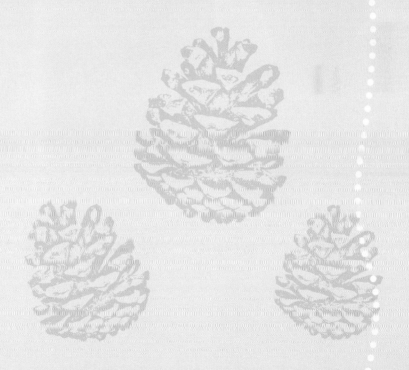

Baby bird nests

In the fall, the flowers and some of the shrubs in the garden start to die back and it is often the best time to go gathering. You can find wonderfully shaped seedpods and dried flower heads that can be transformed into cute animals. Take a look at your collection, even the smallest item may spark off an idea—a spiky dried plant could be a hedgehog, or turn a seedpod into a caterpillar. You may not have the exact same seed head that I have used for these little birds but look around and you will soon find something suitable. The little birds are tiny and half a walnut shell makes a perfect, cozy nest.

Materials

Walnut shells
Paint in assorted colors
Small paintbrush
Template on page 122, tracing
    paper and pencil (optional)
Small piece of colored felt
Scissors
Glue
Dried seed heads
Peppercorns
Dried moss
Small feather

1 Give the outside of the walnut shells a coat of paint. These have been painted in pretty pastel colors. Let dry.

2 Cut a small triangle of felt from the corner of the piece of felt (or use the template on page 122) and dip it into the glue along one edge. Stick the felt triangle onto the seed head for the beak and stick on two peppercorns for the eyes.

3 To give your bird a little character, paint a small white dot on each peppercorn eye.

4 Add a little dried moss to the walnut shell as a bed for your baby bird. Place the little bird in the shell and position a feather behind to add the final flourish.

Shell mice

Here is another way to use the pretty shells you have brought back from a seaside trip. Use different-sized shells to make up a whole family of mice. Don't worry if you can't find the exact shells that I have used, experiment with the shells that you have—the mice may turn out a little different but will be just as cute!

Materials

Assorted shells
Glue
String
Scissors
Raffia
Black marker pen

1 Glue a pointed shell onto a shell you have chosen as the body. You may have to hold the shells in position for a few minutes to let the glue dry.

2 Stick the ears in position. A double shell is ideal but don't worry if you don't have one—two similarly sized shells work just as well. Hold the shells in place while the glue sets.

3 Cut a small piece of string for the tail and glue it in position on the underside of the body.

4 Cut some small pieces of raffia and stick them under the nose to make the whiskers. Finally, draw on some little black eyes.

Pine cone bugs

Pine cones, in all shapes and sizes, are one of my favorite finds on a woodland walk. I have a bowl of them that I have painted white and silver for Christmas, and plain ones strung onto ribbon for a festive garland. They also make a great base for these weird and wonderful bug-eyed critters. Use a selection of seed heads, acorns, leaves, and bark to make up all the other bug parts.

Materials

Waxed beading thread or
   colored string
Scissors
Pine cones, twigs, leaves, bark,
   dried flowers
Small pieces of colored felt
Glue

1 Cut three lengths of thread or string, about 8in (20cm) long. Tie a knot in each end for the feet. Attach to the pine cone by tying around the middle, leaving the ends dangling down for the bug's legs.

2 Find something suitable from your woodland selection for the eye stalks—I have used the inner part of two pine cones. Glue them in position.

3 Cut out some small circles of felt to make the eyes, gluing a smaller circle in a contrasting color to the center for the pupil. Glue them in position on the eye stalks.

4 For the wings, squeeze a couple of blobs of glue along the back of the pine cone and slot in some leaves and pieces of bark. To suspend your bug, simply tie a piece of string or ribbon around its middle.

Pebble pets

I love collecting pebbles on the beach—there is always one that catches my eye, especially when they are wet and shiny. One of our favorite beachcombing games is who can find the best face on a pebble. Look out for ones with holes, they make great ready-made eyes or smiles. Add some arms, legs, or hair and you have an instant, adorable pebble pal. Cute or scary, each one will have its own character.

Materials

Felt in assorted colors
Pebbles
Glue
Scissors
Plain white paper
Colored felt-tip pens

1 Cut out a selection of felt feet, arms, and hair in different colored felt. Look carefully at your pebbles: one may look like a dragon, so you could cut some spines for it; another may look like an alien, so you may want to give it some eyes on stalks.

2 Using a dark-colored pen, draw some small circles for eyes on white paper. Cut out the eyes and stick them onto your pet.

3 Attach the felt arms, legs, and hair with glue. You may need to hold the felt in place while the glue starts to set.

Words of wisdom

Use some scraps of wool to make funky hairstyles. Pipe cleaners in bright colors would also make great arms and legs—you can bend the wire to make hands and feet.

Pebble owl family

This little family of owls has a fun retro look about it, painted with bright decorative patterns. You can use acrylic paints or brush pens, which you may find easier to control on small areas. When looking for the right pebble, try to find ones with flat bottoms so they can stand up on their own. Pick out pebbles of different sizes to make up a whole family.

Materials

Smooth pebble
White acrylic paint
Paintbrush
Template on page 122,
  tracing paper and
  pencil (optional)
Colored paints or felt-tip
  brush pens
Varnish

1 Make sure your pebble is clean and dry. Decide which side is going to be the front of the owl and paint it with a base coat of white. Let dry.

2 Paint or draw on your owl. It is easiest to start with the eyes. Use lots of bright colors. I have made the eyes in flower shapes for a retro look. (If you wish, copy the template on page 122.)

3 Paint in some wings and decorate with spots, stripes, or flowers. The brighter the better!

4 Finally, if you like, you can give your owl a coat of varnish for extra shine. Make a few more owls in the same way and when everything is dry, line them up on a bedroom shelf to keep watch.

Mini fairy garden

As a child, one of my favorite pastimes was to make tiny gardens. I even made mini tables and chairs, with the table set with miniature plates of food made from leaves and seeds. This garden is very special, with a little winding path leading to a group of tiny houses. Let your imagination go wild and use twigs, pebbles, and moss to decorate and create your own enchanted fairy world.

Materials

Bark, pine cones, twigs
Glue
Paint in assorted colors
Paintbrush
Flowerpot or a suitable container
Plants and potting compost
Pebbles, pieces of slate, nutshells

1 To make the fairy houses, start with a piece of bark. Try to break it so that it has a point at one end for the roof. Pull off some of the outer sections of a pine cone and stick them down in rows to form roof tiles.

2 Continue to glue on pieces of pine cone or dried leaves to make the top section of the roof and the doors and windows.

Words of wisdom

Why not make an extra mini garden to place on a kitchen windowsill? Use a jar, small flowerpot, or even an egg carton, and plant cress and other small herbs that you can actually use.

3 Paint some of the roof tiles in shades of orange and paint the doors, roof, and curtains in the windows. If you wish, make a few more houses.

4 To make the picket fence, break up a few twigs to a similar length. Paint them white all over and lay them in a row. When the paint is dry, glue one twig across the others to finish the fence.

5 Cut toadstool shapes from thin bark and then paint them in red and white. Let the paint dry before adding little dots of white to the red top.

6 Now for the really fun part! Build up your garden by arranging small plants in some potting compost in a flowerpot or suitable container. If you put living plants in your container, you can watch your fairy garden develop and grow.

7 Between the plants add little areas of pebbles, slate pathways, and a pond made from a nutshell .

8 Finally, place the fairy houses, fence, and toadstools in position amongst the plants and wait for the fairy folk to move in.

Items to collect chart

In the forest:

Deciduous leaves

Evergreen leaves

Twigs

Conkers

Acorns

Seed heads

Pine cones

Grasses

Nuts

Hop heads

In the garden:

Flower pots

Twigs

Dried flowers

Daisies

Pebbles

Larger stones

Buttercups

Daisies

Dandelions

On the beach:

Sand

Shells

Driftwood

Pebbles

Rope

Seaweed

Sea-washed glass

In the home:

Orange peel

Lemon peel

Melon peel

Peach stone

Plastic bags

Scrap fabric and ribbons

Leaves from pot plants

Dried flowers

Peppercorns

Nuts

Templates

All the templates are shown at full size, so you won't need to enlarge them to use on your creations. For many projects you need to transfer the template onto paper or cardstock, using tracing paper. Place a sheet of tracing paper over the template and secure with some masking tape. Trace the lines with a hard 4 (2H) pencil, then turn the tracing paper over and go over the lines again on the reverse with a softer pencil, such as a 2 (HB). Now turn the tracing paper over again and place it in position on your chosen paper or cardstock. Go over all the lines carefully with the 4 (2H) pencil, and then remove the tracing paper. This will give you a nice, clear outline.

Don't worry if you can't find some of the items required to make the projects. They might be out of season or not grow in your region so we have provided some templates that you can use to replace those hard to find materials. While the illustrations on some of the projects are just an example of what you can draw, we've also supplied templates if you want to copy the ones in the photographs. Try to draw them yourselves though, it's a lot more fun if you create something all on your own!

Pressed flower butterfly
Petal and flower templates
page 24

Pressed flower butterfly
Petal and flower templates
page 24

Hanging bird decoration
Wing and beak templates
page 39

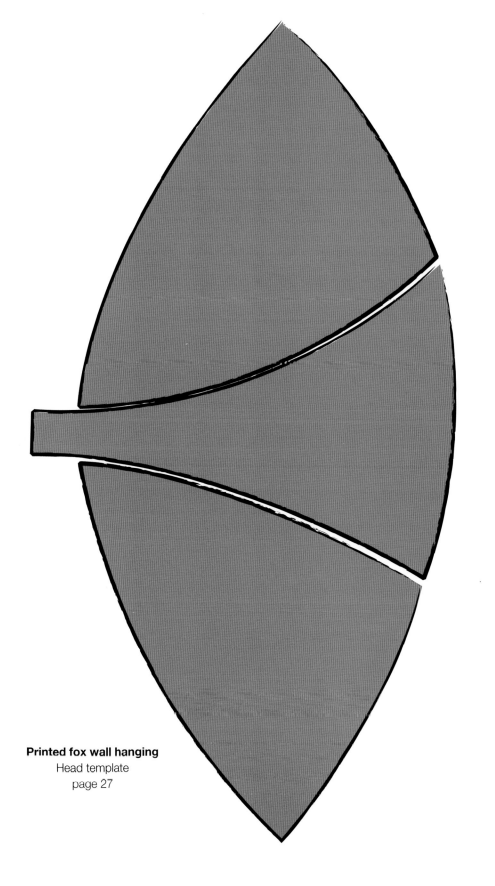

Printed fox wall hanging
Head template
page 27

Box frame seaside scene
House template
page 33

Templates **117**

Character eyes, noses, and mouths to draw onto your creatures.
Try them on the following projects:
Froggy bookends (page 40)
Driftwood odd bunch (page 94)
Pine-cone bugs (page 105)
Pebble pets (page 106)

Aboriginal bark bowl
Lizard template
page 42

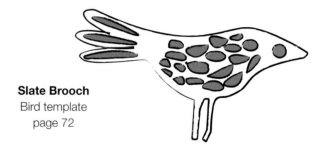

Leaf print Easter eggs
Leaf template
page 46

Slate Brooch
Bird template
page 72

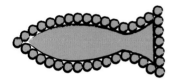

Shell pendant
Fish and skull templates
page 75

Daisy print bags
Daisy template
page 71

Fern print gift wrap and garland
Bird gift tag template
page 76

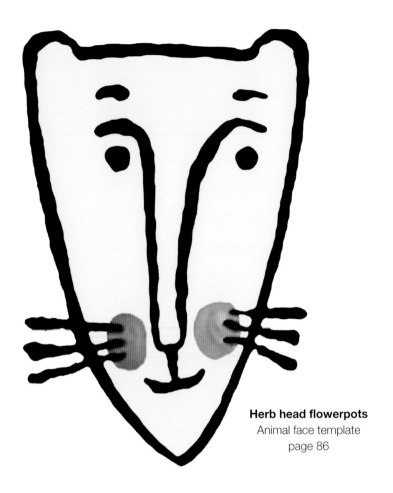

Herb head flowerpots
Animal face template
page 86

Flower family
Dog template
page 89

Baby bird nests
Beak template
page 100

Pebble owl family
Owl template
page 108

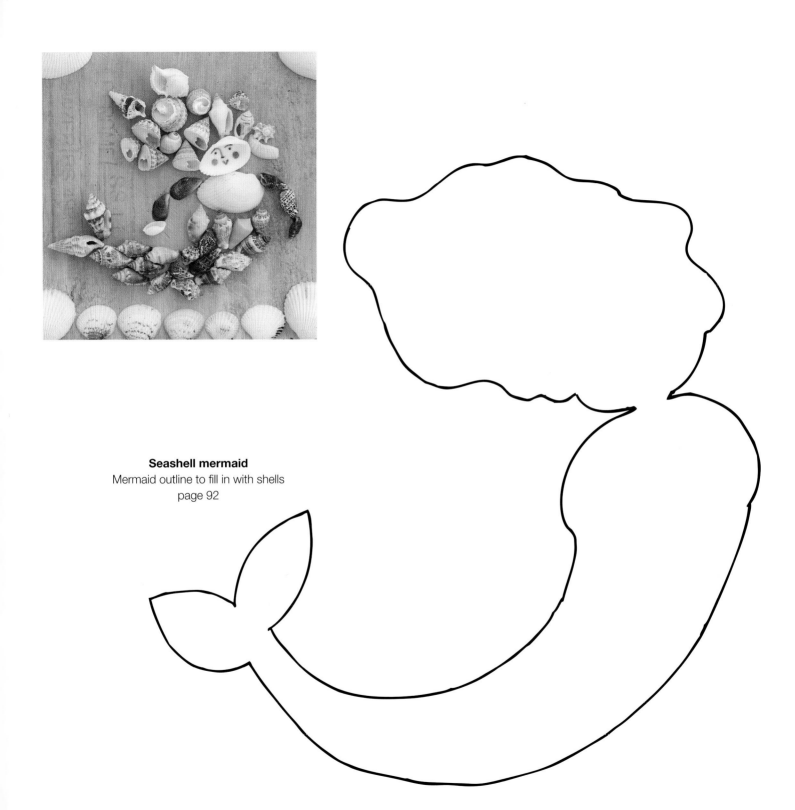

Seashell mermaid
Mermaid outline to fill in with shells
page 92

Suppliers

US

Art Supplies Online
800-967-7367
www.artsuppliesonline.com

Craft Site Directory
Useful online resource
www.craftsitedirectory.com

Crafts etc.
800-888-0321
www.craftsetc.com

Create For Less
866-333-4463
www.createforless.com

Creative Kids Crafts
510-364-2369
www.creativekidscrafts.com

Darice
866-432-7423
www.darice.com

Hobby Lobby
Stores nationwide
www.hobbylobby.com

Jo-ann Fabric & Crafts
888-739-4120
www.joann.com

Kids Craft Supplies
866-777-8654
www.kidscraftsupplies.com

Michaels
Stores nationwide
www.michaels.com

S&S Worldwide Craft Supplies
800-288-9941
www.ssww.com

Sunshine Crafts
800-729-2878
www.sunshinecrafts.com

Toys "R" Us
Stores nationwide
www.toysrus.com

UK

Early Learning Centre
08705 352 352
www.elc.co.uk

Homecrafts Direct
0116 269 7733
www.homecrafts.co.uk

Hobbycraft
0800 027 2387
www.hobbycraft.co.uk

John Lewis
08456 049 049
www.johnlewis.co.uk

Kidzcraft
01793 327022
www.kidzcraft.co.uk

Paperchase
0161 839 1500 for
mail order
www.paperchase.co.uk

Paper and String
www.paper-and-string.co.uk

Index

Acknowledgments

I would like to thank all at CICO for giving me the opportunity to write this book. A special thanks to Cindy, Pete, and Sally. Thanks to the designer, Jacqui Caulton, who has created such a fun and stylish looking book. Thanks to Claire Richardson for her wonderful photography and for Ellie for all her help so late in her pregnancy! Thanks to all our models, all of whom worked like true professionals! Aiden, Alice, Che, Flora, Freya, Harry, Harvey, Honaka, Keo, Lola, Orla, and Rosy. Thank you to Bill and Jo for letting me use their amazing garden. Thanks to Karen, Gilbert, Birdie, and Edie for joining me on many a foraging trip! Finally, as always, a special thanks to my family, Ian, Milly, Florence, Henrietta, and Harvey for all their encouragement and support.